Discovering
OLD BICYCLES

T. E. Crowley

Shire Publications Ltd

CONTENTS

ACKNOWLEDGEMENTS

Invaluable help was received from the following: J. Boulton, R. F. Cumberland, Wing Commander T. E. Guttery and C. N. Passey.

Photographs are acknowledged as follows: Passey Collection, plates 1, 4, 8, 9, 10, 11, 13, 19, 21, 22, 24, 25, 27, 28; Crown Copyright, Science Museum, London, plates 2, 5, 12; lent to the Science Museum by W. J. Carey Esq., photo Science Museum, London, plate 6; Shuttleworth Collection, plates 3, 17, 23; courtesy of *Cycling*, plates 7, 20; Pinkerton Collection, plate 14; J. Bone Collection, plate 15; C. Slemeck, plate 26.

The cover photograph taken c. 1885 shows a penny-farthing, probably made in the U.S.A.

1. WHAT ARE BIKES FOR ?

The spirit of cycling is very much alive in most of the countries of the world, and it looks as though it will continue that way for a long time to come, certainly as long as there are active people wishing to travel about in the most convenient and inexpensive way imaginable. It would be almost impossible to compute the number of bicycles in existence— certainly several millions in this country alone, and this represents a major industry in which Great Britain through the years has always played the leading part.

Cycling is, of course, more than just a means of transport. Enthusiasts there are in plenty, people determined to get the most out of the sport and hobby, experts in such matters as time trials, track racing, cyclo-cross or long-distance touring, usually willing to spend money on specially built and very expensive machines and accessories. Many cycling activities the general public sees and hears very little about because the enthusiasts are far outnumbered by the typical every-day cyclist—somebody going to work or into the village for shopping, a small child being taken to a nursery school in a pillion chair or a delivery boy with a laden tradesman's bicycle. The machines are sometimes ill-fitting, often too large or too small, and the riders have made no attempt to adjust them. They may be in poor condition and neglected. It is frequently evident that the rider has taught himself to ride and done it rather badly, with no expert advice. All this is minor; the bicycle serves them all with extraordinary economy, efficiency and safety. Misused and neglected over periods of many years, it is still usually able to carry out its functions without much trouble, and few inventions have been so beneficial to mankind.

Although variations and improvements are always being thought out in the name of better efficiency (or even of sales publicity), for practical purposes the design of the bicycle, like that of the saucepan and the yard-broom, reached finality three generations or so ago, further back than can be remembered by the oldest among us.

It is a very usual thing that when an invention attains an effective finality of design, it is swept entirely away by some newer concept employing quite different principles. The great windjammers took two thousand years to reach perfection, and within a generation they were gone. Eight or nine hundred years saw the rise and sudden disappearance of the wind and water mills, a hundred and fifty years sufficed for the steam engine, but in each case their overthrow, as a feature of day-to-day living, was just as sudden and total. Many other examples will occur to the reader; it happened with manual sewing machines and may happen with manual typewriters; it is to be hoped that it will happen soon with diesel engines.

The cycle however, is a striking exception. Basic design became static when all alternatives had been explored and found wanting. Detail improvements naturally continued but nothing has supplanted or is likely to supplant the conventional design, and it is almost impossible to determine even to ten years (and probably to twenty) the age of a cycle merely by looking at it.

Popularity

The popularity of bicycles has been affected by various factors but probably not by stagnation of design, because sufficient varieties have always been available to satisfy the need for different styles and patterns, and it is usually possible to maintain public interest by skilfully advertised changes in appearance or decoration. The one thing which militates against cycling is the motor-car which, with its superior weight and protection, its noise, speed and smell, can when in sufficient quantity remove most of the pleasure from cycling. Inconsiderate motorists are comparatively very few, but if they may be thought of as one per cent of all passing cars, it does not take long for a hundred cars to go by, so that life on a busy road can be less than pleasant for the cyclist. In addition, some motorists have insufficient imagination fully to understand the possible extra difficulties encountered by the cyclist on a wet and windy night or in frozen slush. Bicycles do not form part of that traffic for which extra roads are planned and built: they are considered very little by some planning engineers and hence it can be noticed that where motor traffic is heaviest, cycles are fewest. Cars have increased in speed to the point where the average driver is hard put to it to control the performance at his disposal, and if anything unusual happens at modern speeds, reaction time, more often than not, may be inadequate to deal with the situation. Cycle speeds have not increased—leg power is the same as it always was—and single-track vehicles are sometimes not too easily seen by drivers whose main problems concern coping with other cars. The cyclist is often made uncomfortably aware that he or she is between the millstones, and even though an extra mile or two is of greater importance to him than to the motorist, he tends to seek the quieter roads when he can. To this extent, the sport and pastime is driven into a corner, but the influence is unlikely to be a critical one. The term 'push-bike', with its once faintly deprecatory and apologetic overtones, has come in the passage of years to wear a prouder air and to suggest a superior activity which the inactive comfort-lover is incapable of sharing.

If, as has been said, design has remained almost unchanged this century, just as with saucepans, is there any need for a history book on either? The answer is that both can provide an extraordinarily interesting story of progress and a very human insight into the working of men's minds. Most people can recall pictures of boneshakers and penny-farthings, but there is a great deal more to it than this; designs flourished in extraordinary variety and ingenuity, but nearly always with some flaw which sooner or later eliminated them. The mainstream emerged comparatively late and was perfected in, at most, ten years; but people were provided with interest, fun and usefulness all along the way.

2. THE HOBBY-HORSE: UP TO 1850

Nobody knows who invented the wheel or the arch; everybody thinks he knows who invented the railway engine and the telephone. It is, however, not nearly as simple as that, and reading about the lives of famous inventors, one soon comes to the conclusion that very often what they did was to gather together the work of those who went before them, to review other people's unused ideas and to develop to a greater or lesser extent what was already potentially in existence. The original concept often came centuries before but was not, or could not then be developed, and so lay dormant until the fertilising mind rediscovered it. Leonardo da Vinci's proposals for flying machines form a good example. The techniques to transform his ideas into practice did not exist until centuries later, but who else can be named as the inventor of the flying machine?

This is the case with the bicycle. Nobody can be said to have invented it although several people constructed machines which represented great steps forward or embodied principles not previously employed. Historical research, however, generally seems to show that those principles had been suggested years before in one way or another, but never developed at the time. The 'boneshaker' or velocipede might have been put

on the market fifty years before it was, had there been anyone
around perceptive enough to pick up and develop all the
hints that were available at that time. Thus, although the
first hobby-horses (from which all bicycles are descended)
appeared in Paris in 1816, there is a stained-glass window in
Stoke Poges church depicting a cherub blowing a trumpet
and seated on what to all appearances is a hobby-horse;
and the date is 1642. Again, although there is no record
of a bicycle ever having been driven by cranks and pedals
turning the front wheel before 1865, there exists a scurrilous
cartoon of the Prince Regent, presumably intended as usual
to be in a condition of semi-drunkenness, lying full length
on a hobby-horse with his hands on cranks attached to the
front wheel. The date was fifty years before anyone thought
of using the idea.

From about 1760 onwards, there are records of four-wheel
carriages steered by one man, presumably the owner, and
driven by a footman behind, throwing his weight alternately
on a pair of footboards connected to the wheels by a ratchet
mechanism. Probably progress would have been as good had
he dismounted and merely pushed the whole contraption
along, but a number of such quadricycles were unquestionably
made, and it raises the important point—how to define a cycle.
Many cycles in the 1870-1885 era were designed to be propelled
by one person and steered by another and thus, by definition,
one can hardly exclude bath-chairs or invalid chairs from the
world of cycles, however many wheels they have. The
available forms of modern lightweight invalid chairs indeed
are so well designed and so mobile that they are capable of
much that befits a contemporary tricycle.

1816 brought a contraption to Paris which aroused
considerable interest. Nicéphore Niepce, one of the 'fathers
of photography', had a great deal to do with it, and he got
the idea from a two-wheeled toy for grown-ups invented by
de Sivrac in Paris in 1791 and used by some of the dandies
of the time. They named it the Célérifère, but Niepce
called his new version the Céléripede, and it consisted of
two wooden wheels joined by a beam with handles on which
to rest the hands. Early models were not even steerable,
but the thing was rapidly improved upon by Baron Drais
de Saverbrunn of Mannheim, who added a rest for the arms
while holding the steering rod and called it the 'Draisienne'.
It became popular for a while both in France and England
(both patents date from 1818), and was produced in numbers
in this country by Dennis Johnson, coachmaker, of Long
Acre, under the name of the 'Pedestrian Curricle', a title

which was very soon dropped in favour of the 'hobby-horse' or 'dandy-horse'; by 1819 hundreds were being sold to fashionable young bloods who strode madly through the mud on them, wearing out their boot-leather (plate 1). A ladies' model was also available. The idea as it stood was obviously sterile, and despite one or two tentative and abortive ideas for driving the machines by elaborate lever arrangements, by 1830 the hobby-horse was dead and forgotten except by one or two eccentrics. It had led to nothing.

No thoughts seem to have been devoted to the design of two-wheel transport for another decade, but some quite practical light four-wheeled vehicles propelled by foot treadles and steered by 'reins' were constructed and sold commercially for a number of years: in fact no fewer than three manufacturers exhibited at the Great Exhibition of 1851, and one example was made for the Prince Consort. Several still exist.

Momentarily, the bicycle

It was, however, in 1839 that a blacksmith of Courthill, Dumfriesshire, Kirkpatrick Macmillan (1810-1878), devised and built a simple scheme for driving a boneshaker by pedal action instead of by walking (plate 2). His pedals consisted of swinging levers connected to crankpins on the rear axle by long rods. He had the engineering instinct to see the benefit of an inclined front fork, and he fitted a brake worked via a cord twisted round the handlebars. The machine was undoubtedly practical and the inventor paid several visits to Glasgow, forty miles away, with its help. He claimed no patents, and the layout was copied and improved in various details by other Scottish craftsmen, notably Gavin Dalzell (1811-1863) of Lesmahagow, Lanark-shire, who in 1846 handsomely beat the Royal Mail coach for a wager, riding round it three times. These primitive designs undoubtedly pointed out the way ahead but the astonishing thing is that they were not developed or refined —the whole idea was allowed to drop once more, and when later designs became popular they were greatly inferior in concept. Apart from one or two abortive efforts to design a useful tricycle, no further interest seems to have been taken in the subject at least for another fifteen or twenty years.

3. THE BONESHAKER

The early 1860s brought an increase of interest once more, and a few drawings which still remain show that various people were considering the problems of cranks and levers or chain drives to propel two- and three-wheeled vehicles. Some inventors seemed to be at the stage of trying merely to improve the hobby-horse; however, when a bicycle did appear it was driven by pedals attached direct to the front-wheel spindle. This was first done experimentally in 1861, and put on the market a little later by Pierre Michaux (1813-1883) and his son Ernest, perambulator makers of Paris. The machine was known as the Velocipède and possessed an iron frame, iron-tyred wheels with wooden spokes like the carts of the day, vertical front fork and a primitive brake applied by cord by twisting the handlebars. The actual inventor is not known with certainty, since the credit was claimed by the chief mechanic of the firm, Pierre Lallement, who took out patents and sold them later to Michaux. He left his employment (apparently in dissatisfaction with his treatment) in 1866, and went to manufacture velocipedes in the USA, but he seems to have had little business acumen and returned to Paris within a year or two to set up in opposition to his old firm. Later years found him back in employment in America.

By 1865 the Michaux type of bicycle was well established and production was running at about four hundred per annum. In 1866 one example was exported to England and bought by Rowley B. Turner, who was connected with the Coventry Sewing Machine Company. He was able to interest the company in producing the Velocipède, mainly for export to France; however, before the arrangements were complete, the Franco-Prussian War had broken out which completely stopped the development of the bicycle in France and encouraged it in this country, at the same time rescuing the city of Coventry from a period of depression.

The 'frustrated exports' were put on the British market and immediately became known as 'boneshakers'. They are said to be distinguishable from the French model by the fact that the pedals were non-adjustable and made triangular in section, but such ideas are not dependable since many examples were locally made to individual order.

The boneshaker develops

James Starley (1801-1881), in many ways the father of the British cycle industry, was foreman at the Coventry works, and introduced various improvements as time went on, including raked forks and a backstep. Within a year or two there were other manufacturers in the field, tricycles could be had, and even a ladies' model, designed with offset wheels to be ridden sidesaddle. Other improvements arrived: solid rubber strips were cemented to the wheels in 1868, the saddle was moved further forward in an effort to get the weight more nearly above the pedals, and the handlebars became wider and higher. The first cycle race was held in Paris in 1868 and was won by an Englishman, James Moore, who proved almost unbeatable for the next few years.

Michaux sold out in 1869 and after the war the purchasers, Compagnie Parisienne, continued to produce improved velocipedes as late as 1891.

1869 was the date of the first permanent British race track, the one at the Crystal Palace. The sport and industry of cycling were on their way forward. New ideas and new principles now appeared in such rapid succession that it is not easy to keep track of them all. Some can have had no hopes of popularity or commercial success, but that did not seem to prevent them from being manufactured and offered to the public. One ingenious gentleman, for instance, produced a monocycle with a seat mounted each side of a single large wheel. Each rider had a pair of handlebars and a pair of pedals. Mounting and dismounting such an arrangement would seem to pose a problem. Several designs of 'dicycle' appeared, notably one by BSA, incorporating two large-diameter wheels joined by an axle on which was fixed a saddle; the driver grasped two steering rods which were arranged to tighten or slacken one or other of the two driving bands through which the leg-power was transmitted from pedal cranks, thus encouraging the machine to go approximately in the direction desired.

In Germany the Michaux bicycle was converted into a tricycle by the building on of a rear axle with a wheel each side of the driver. This dated from 1870, but the ladies' velocipede slightly antedated it, a design involving a drive by cranks and long rods to the twin rear wheels, a steerable front wheel of very small size and a comfortable bucket seat. The thing seemed to be popularly recognised as a self-propelled bath-chair.

9

The Phantom

A great step forward was taken in the seminal year 1869 by the appearance at the Crystal Palace track on 27th May of the Phantom bicycle, produced by Reynolds & Mays (plate 5). Although this looked very like the orthodox bone-shaker at first glance, a closer inspection showed it to be hinged in the middle of the frame, with a link system which resulted in the steering being shared between both wheels. This actually proved to be no improvement at all, and the arrangement never became popular, but the important thing about the Phantom was its use of wire instead of wood for the spokes. The constructors realised that the axles, instead of being supported by thick wooden spokes in compression, could with advantage be suspended by light wire spokes in tension. The wire was attached to one side of the hub, taken up through an iron eye in the rim and back to the other side of the hub. The latter was made in two sections which could be wedged apart after building the wheel, thus providing the necessary tension in the wire. The wheel was provided with a thick rubber tyre cemented on. It was such a big and obvious improvement on the art of the traditional wheelwright that within three years the wooden spoked wheel was seen no more and the wire wheel with radial spokes went through a period of rapid development before the final standardisation of the screwed nipple in the rim, the obvious and effective way of ensuring the correct degree of tension. An example of a transitional form was the arrangement employed on the Ariel bicycle (plate 6) and others, which had cantilever pieces from the hub with wingnuts capable of providing tension in the spokes by moving the rim in a circular direction relative to the hub. This in turn probably led to the idea of the tangent spoke which is in universal use today.

By the year 1869 the bicycle had received its present name, although the term tricycle had been known long before. The first cycle show and concours in this country was held at Fountains Abbey in Yorkshire on 26th June 1869, and certainly did much to popularise the movement; cyclists proceeded to appear quite thickly on the roads, although the pastime was admittedly confined to the young and athletic. The boneshaker continued in fairly general use for a few more years but it had little further potentiality for development as such, and improved types of two- and three-wheeler came on the market in increasing variety from 1870 onwards. John Keen of Surbiton fitted boneshaker wheels with rubber tyres a good two inches thick but even with these, the discomfort of riding one of these machines over the cobbles in towns and the potholes in country roads is almost unimaginable. Tarmac was still thirty-five years ahead. In 1869 an attempt was made to establish a record time for a journey from London to Brighton, but the rider gave up through sheer exhaustion at Redhill. A later and better prepared effort returned a time of sixteen hours, which was halved a few months later.

4. CYCLES GO ALL-METAL

One of the many disadvantages of the boneshaker was the low 'gearing'. This meant that the rider had to pedal rapidly in order to proceed even slowly. This was a necessity when the machines were so heavy, but wire-spoked wheels opened the way for iron rims, crescent-shaped in section to receive a solid rubber tyre, and the saving in weight was considerable. Designers began to think in terms of higher gearing, but so long as the motive power was applied through pedals attached to the front spindle, the only way of attaining this was by increasing the size of the front wheel. Thus was born the idea of the 'penny-farthing', or 'ordinary' as it was called in more dignified circles.

The first advance in this direction seems to have been made by James Starley who, with his colleague William Hillman, invented the Ariel bicycle in 1870. This model was marketed with great publicity, and its introduction was celebrated by both the inventors cycling on it from London to Coventry in one day. This unprecedented event occurred in September 1871, just thirty-seven years before Hillman founded the motor factory which bore his name. The bicycles had iron frames and wheels fitted with the tangential spokes already mentioned, which were one of Starley's inventions, and with a front fork taken right up to a short handlebar. The front wheel had a diameter of about 48 inches and the rear about half that figure. Much the same principles were employed by W. H. Grout, 1871, who patented hollow tubes for forks, tyres vulcanised to the rims and a simpler wheel construction with spokes screwed into nipples threaded through the rim. He called his design the 'Tension' and made a great point of a specially designed pedal, laying down for the first time the principle that a bicycle should be driven by the ball of the foot and not by the instep—a discovery

11

that many people a hundred years later have yet to make.

Both Starley and Grout improved their wheel designs within a couple of years, and Starley marketed a 'speed-gear' which revolved the front wheel at twice the speed of the crank spindle. In 1873 also he designed the Spider bicycle with many detailed improvements to frame and wheels; this model was manufactured by the Coventry Machinists Company, then a very big firm, and its success stimulated Starley to introduce the first true tangentially spoked wheel, in which each spoke points well to one side of the hub instead of to its centre; this came out in 1874.

James Starley

The inventor was a man so prolific of good ideas that a little more should be said about him. James Starley (1831-1881) was born at Albourne near Brighton, where his descendants still live, and started work on his father's farm at the age of eleven. His natural talent for invention soon made itself felt in such things as a new kind of rat-trap. While still a youth he walked to London and gained employment as a gardener to John Penn, the famous marine engineer, and he is recorded as inventing a 'duck balance', a device which allowed the resident ducks to pass from the garden to the Ravensbourne river but prevented rats from coming the reverse way. He contrived a self-rocking cradle and an automatic window, and took opportunities of learning clock and watch making and the repair of umbrellas, sewing machines and musical instruments.

1861 found Starley in Coventry, foreman in the Coventry Sewing Machine Company's factory, and there he introduced some notable improvements in design. The company grew, and in 1868 started to produce the Michaux type of velocipede, changing its name to the Coventry Machinists Company. As was to be expected, Starley disapproved of the design of these boneshakers; he was quick to introduce the mounting-step and followed up by introducing the new-type wheels, as previously mentioned. He was a great believer in tricycles and was probably the first engineer to fit a differential, although he disclaimed the invention of the device.

The company was fortunate in employing an exceptional team of ingenious men at this time, and its prosperity under the guidance of Starley rapidly restored to prosperity the city which had been suffering a bad trade depression. Other cycle manufacturers benefited also, because some of his ideas

Starley refused to patent, and these included the chain-driven tricycle. Before he died, as well as afterwards, he was widely known as the 'Father of the Cycle Industry' and in 1884, only three years after his death, a statue was erected to his memory in Coventry.

By 1873, then, the industry was in a flourishing state and new firms appeared in some number. Among these were Keen of Surbiton who built higher and lighter machines than had previously been achieved, and Dan Rudge, landlord of the Tiger's Head Inn at Wolverhampton, who within a year or so, after a detailed study of the mechanics of cycling, produced one of the first full-sized ordinary (or penny-farthing) bicycles.

5. THE PENNY-FARTHING

As with Beefeaters, the undignified but descriptive name 'Penny-farthing' for a dignified object, is so generally understood and accepted that it will not be denied. The design of these machines was so distinctive and their use became so popular, that they are generally associated more than any other type with the history of the bicycle in the high Victorian age. There is no doubt that it became a cult among its riders, partly because its use was restricted to the young and athletic, and partly because there was a certain amount of difficulty and occasionally even some danger in its successful management. Falls, especially on the villainous roads of the day, were frequent, and as the greatest leg power was obtainable only if the saddle was positioned as nearly as possible vertically over the front spindle, the whole machine was somewhat unstable and could be upset by a comparatively small obstruction in the road. At the same time, by its lights the design was extremely efficient. Frictional losses were at a minimum (four bearings only), the machines were made to measure and therefore fitted well, and the large front wheel minimised road shocks considerably, as any large wheel will always do. Another advantage to the Victorian mind was that the riders, at any rate while they remained vertical, had a most dignified appearance.

Wheel size, on which the speed of rotation of the pedals was naturally dependent, was made as large as possible and this for a tall man could reach 60 inches in diameter; such machines were provided with up to three backsteps for mounting purposes, and cranks of various lengths were available. Accessories were not in much demand, although some riders hung an oil lamp from the front hub, swinging by means of a leather strap and providing a non-obligatory warning of approach.

Of all the many varieties of bicycle and tricycle offered to the public in the eighties, there is no doubt that the 'high ordinary' was the most popular and, in spite of its disadvantages, the most practical for the conditions of the day. It was supposed to have been invented by Magee of Paris in 1869; many new companies were formed within a year or two to build these machines (in 1874 there were over twenty in this country), and although some of these were short-lived, they were replaced during the following decade by more substantial concerns which earned for themselves lasting reputations.

1874 was the year of the Ladies' Ordinary, designed under the Ariel brand name by James Starley, to be ridden side-saddle. This might be thought of as a case where engineers refuse to accept the impossible and indeed the success of the design does not seem to have been marked. The pedals operated the front-wheel cranks through levers, the track of the front wheel was offset, and one handlebar was longer than the other to counteract the bias of the riding position. It does not sound very comfortable.

The penny-farthing became so fashionable during the mid seventies that it seemed to inhibit for a while the production of other designs, and people unable to attain to 'ordinary' height were very badly catered for; practically no tricycles of any sort were being manufactured and, with the important exception of Lawson's bicycle (to be described later), no 'safety' bicycles either until at least 1878, when the market started to diversify once more.

Following through the development of the ordinary we find that, as time went on, machines were improved and lightened: in fact it was not long before extra-light racing models were available, some of them of almost unbelievable attenuation. In 1876 for instance, John Keen, a racing specialist, brought out a model with a stub axle for the rear wheel, thus saving the weight of half a fork; and in the same year most makers went over to the 'Stanley' steering head, very akin to the modern pattern, in place of the old-fashioned and awkward socket head. Ball bearings were introduced in 1877 and at first were of many strange types including one invented by the Starleys, using dumb-bell shaped rollers spaced apart by smaller plain rollers. Rudge patented a double-cone ball bearing about the same time, with the balls running on a central sleeve and therefore having three-point contact. By 1879 almost all bicycles were fitted with ball bearings in place of brass bushes, and the improvement in running was of course considerable.

Bayliss-Thomas, later to use the Excelsior trademark, were in the market in 1879 with a design using hollow drawn front forks, and it was at about this time that the ordinary may be said to have reached its greatest popularity. The Matchless, produced by the Collier brothers in 1880, offered a still further reduction in weight through the adoption of steel tubing for frame and forks, and of hollow wheel rims. The Rudge of 1884, winner of many international races, weighed under twenty-two pounds. Singer marketed miniature penny-farthings for children as well as more orthodox models, but with all the variety offered to the public it was becoming obvious that the ordinary was satisfying less and less of the potential demand for wheeled transport, the market was diversifying once more, and by 1892-3 the manufacture of the penny-farthing had ceased.

Ordinary variations

Discontent with the restrictions imposed by the design of the ordinary seemed to find sudden outlet in 1878 with a crop of new designs of both bicycle and tricycle. First of all designers began to see that if the pedalling gear could be arranged to drive the front axle indirectly, by means of pivoted connecting rods, the pedals might be mounted a good way below the front axle and behind it. This would in effect place them further under the rider so that his weight would be made more effective, the size of the front wheel could be reduced and the forks could be raked backwards. This change improved both steering and safety but at the expense of increased complexity; the machines proved somewhat slow.

Some confusion existed at the time about the name to be given to this new class of machine; some writers referred to them as 'dwarf ordinaries' and others, less accurately but with a better sense of publicity, as 'high safeties'. In fact the safety bicycle was necessarily a rear-driven model as we shall see.

The first two 'dwarf' designs were named the Facile (plate 16) and the Xtra-ordinary, the latter made by Singer (plate 11). The layout in each case was quite different but the principle was the same, employing pivoted rocking pedals linked to cranks on the axle. Following these, the advantages of gearing became obvious as the front-wheel size declined; Otto and Wallis reduced the wheel to 36 inches, placed a crank each side on an extension of the front forks, and two chain drives from there to the wheel spindle. The pedals could then be made to revolve at a different rate from the front wheel. The layout was good enough to survive for at least six or seven years and later versions were produced by Hillman Herbert and Cooper under the name of the Kangaroo (plate 17). The gearing proved to have a speed advantage, and the machine gained the one-hundred-mile record in 1884. Soon after this time a neat, self-contained hub gear of sun and planet design was marketed by the Crypto Cycle Co. and incorporated in the Geared Facile dwarf ordinary of 1888, some examples of which were fitted with pneumatic tyres and were employed to capture a number of records (plate 21). By this time, however, the cycling world was marching on and the era of tricycles had arrived.

The last descendant of the ordinary, produced in 1892, was a redesign by the Crypto company and they called it the Bantam (plates 22 and 23). It was driven through a hub gear fitted to a moderate-sized front wheel with forks and frame something like a miniature penny-farthing; pneumatic tyres were fitted. It was a layout of this type which was adapted in 1896 by Colonel (later General Sir) H. Capel Holden to produce the world's first four-cylinder motor-cycle and the first marketable British design.

6. THE TRICYCLE AGE

It is not very practical to review the history of cycle design on a strictly chronological basis because the development of the bicycle proceeded quite independently from that of the tricycle, and the two main types are therefore better dealt with separately. This chapter attempts to deal with the multiplicity of tricycle and quadricycle designs which swarmed on the roads in the eighties. They were all aimed at a market not catered for by the two-wheeler of the day—that is, for older citizens, those more timid or more sedate as well as for people who wanted to travel in company and did not ask for speed. The early machines were in fact distinctly on the heavy side and had to be low-geared accordingly.

Treadle-driven tricycles and boneshakers with three wheels had been built in small numbers between 1850 and 1870 as we have seen, but the public had to wait as late as 1877 for an up-to-date and practical three-wheeler to reach the market. Once again it was James Starley who led the way, with a model which became known as the Coventry Lever, built by Haynes and Jeffreys; this design was a radical departure from anything previously known. To the left of the driver was a 50-inch diameter driving wheel and to his right a long steel tube supporting two 20-inch wheels, one behind the other, and both steered by a bathchair handle. The driving spindle of the big wheel extended under the upholstered seat, where it was bent into double cranks connected to a pair of foot levers. In practice, these proved very awkward and were soon replaced by pedals and a chain drive, which gave better control over the gearing. Steering of the later models was by rack and pinion.

This design set the ball rolling in a new direction and it was rapidly followed by several others. It was marketed on 9th March 1877, and before the end of the same year there was a variety of different makes and patterns to choose from. H. J. Lawson introduced the Coventry Rotary, a similar layout but having cranks with pedals mounted on a bottom bracket, and a chain drive thence to the extended driving-wheel spindle. As this model was further developed, it became known in turn as the Coventry Rudge and in 1880 as the Rudge Rotary, and became a popular and long-lasting make (plate 9). Lawson himself was a most talented and ingenious designer in the cycle field who later transferred his attention to the world of motors and built in the middle nineties an enormous and ramshackle financial empire.

At much the same time as the Coventry Lever there appeared at least two other designs; the Dublin Tricycle mounted a sprung seat on a Y-shaped frame which supported a large driving wheel behind the driver and two small wheels side by side ahead of him. Each of the latter was mounted in a steerable fork and they were connected by a steering bar. The drive was by foot levers connected direct to cranks on the rear wheel. The other design was a true 'manumotive', that is, hand-propelled; this was produced by R. L. Burkett of Wolverhampton and had a slatted seat mounted between two large driving wheels connected by a cranked axle. A small front wheel was steered by a bath-chair handle and the motive power was provided by pulling and pushing this handle, which was connected by a long rod at its lower end to the rear crank. Seen from over the hedge, the rider must have had the appearance of an ataxic oarsman, bobbing wildly to and fro in his meandering progress.

17

Other types were constructed, providing seats for up to eight people. The Beaconsfield, for five, according to a description of the time, was arranged so that the front man rode over the steering wheel and behind him, in a conveyance of ample proportions, sat four men working a swinging bar to and fro by hand. The result, according to a cynical contemporary, was 'akin to eating a bantam's egg with a soup ladle', and the contraption was painfully slow.

In 1879 Starley modified the Coventry Lever by adding another large driving wheel, thus making it into a quadricycle and allowing the arrangement of two seats side by side. Soon after this, the small rear wheel vanished and the result became a front-wheel steering two-seater tricycle (plate 8). Trouble with this model veering from side to side of the road according to the varying exertions of the two riders led to Starley fitting his new bevel gear differential, designed to feed the power equally to the two driving wheels: this was soon adopted by all two-wheel driven vehicles.

1879 also saw the appearance of the Otto Dicycle, of which as many as a thousand were turned out. Two large wheels were joined by an axle having a loop in the centre in which the seat was placed. Pedal cranks transmitted the power independently to each wheel via pulleys and steel belts, and steering was provided by turning a handle and so slackening one of the belts as required—or thereabouts. Manufacture was by BSA.

Tricycle designs that year were many and diverse. The Coventry Machinists' Company produced the Cheylesmore (plate 13), a further development of the Coventry Lever; the Doubleday and Humber sat the rider between two large wheels with a very small one behind and a chain drive. Steering proved heavy and not very accurate, but the model set a fashion. Starley's two-seater side-by-side tricycle which employed the differential was ordered by the Prince of Wales and thereafter became known as the 'Royal Salvo'. It weighed 120lb. Another of Starley's designs was the Compressus, a folding tricycle.

The Singer had a rear wheel driven by lever gearing and two small wheels in front steered by a connecting bar and hand-grip; Excelsior offered a machine with a large driving wheel to the left of the seat, a rather smaller one on the right and a very small steering wheel behind: a sort of penny-halfpenny farthing which they called the 'One-two-three'. The Gnat by Garrard of Uxbridge was similar to the Singer but had all three wheels of almost the same size; the Omnicycle by T. Butler, along the lines of the Royal Salvo, had a speed-varying arrangement consisting of hand-adjusted segments of circles on the axle, which were reciprocated by leather straps attached to the pedal stirrups. This varied the length of the stroke and its effectiveness must have been proved, since the machine won records.

Later tricycles and others

1881 brought the Ideal, built for two, and more popularly known as the Octopus or Hen-and-Chickens. This had one large central wheel with four small ones round it at the corners of a square. The result was a very stable vehicle, an upset was almost impossible, but progress required most of the road width. In theory, when the conveyance was under way, the small wheels were all off the ground; in practice, inequalities in the road often resulted in the driving wheel losing contact, leaving the riders pedalling helplessly in space.

This was the year when box tricycles became available for the delivery of goods, and a monocycle by Pearce made its appearance. This design provided a seat mounted each side of the single wheel, each having its own handlebars, chain and pedals. Of a more practical nature was the Leicester Safety, where the rider sat between two large wheels, chain driven, with a small wheel in front steered indirectly through a long bar. It was nicknamed the 'Humber-turned-round', but it did show the way to the final and most practical layout of tricycle. Quadrant came out with a rear-driven, front-steering tricycle also, notable for a new method of mounting the front steering wheel, from which it derived its name (plate 14). The front wheel was large, and this was found to improve the steering.

Other notable names in the market at this time, each with its own variant of design, included the National, the Premier (Hillman, Herbert and Cooper), the Merlin, the Harrison of Manchester and the Centaur. Dan Rudge of Wolverhampton died on 26th June 1880 and his firm was merged with the Tangent and Coventry Cycle Co. (successors to Haynes and Jeffreys) to form the Rudge Cycle Co. Ltd.

1884 saw the Cripper tricycle, invented by R. Cripps (who won many races on it), and manufactured by Humbers. This was at last a layout providing direct steering of the front wheel held in an inclined front fork and steering-head. Drive was by an enclosed chain to the large twin rear wheels. Within a couple of years this arrangement had ousted nearly all the other layouts including the Humber, and had itself grown three equal wheels 28 inches in diameter; it was known as the 'direct steerer', and tricycle design for the single rider was suddenly crystallised.

There was not much more to be done with wheel or drive arrangements. The success of the Cripper was quickly followed up by the production of a tandem version with a second set of pedals and chain drive to the differential; improvements to the frame design continued. Singers offered a fine tricycle with inclined steering head and curved front fork in 1888, showing that the principles of steering had at last been fully grasped. They were also responsible for the Multi-military Cycle which carried eight, sixteen or more between pairs of wheels coupled together with towbars, and wound its sinuous way along like some monster road-serpent. But not for long. Mechanical millipedes carried whole clubs that year, but like the last and clumsiest of the dinosaurs, they proceeded on their way only to oblivion.

A popular design suitable for both touring and racing was the 'Olympia' produced by Marriott and Cooper; this might be called the last of the variants, having two large front steering wheels, two seats and a large rear driving wheel. 1890 brought the Invincible tandem tricycle with one rider perched to the rear of the twin rear driving wheels; by 1893 the great Bidlake had set up a paced twenty-four hour tricycle record of over 410 miles, unbeaten for sixty years; but tricycling was declining, and by the mid nineties it had been quite superseded in popularity by the ease and lightness of the safety bicycle.

7. THE VICTORY OF THE SAFETY

The layout of the ordinary bicycle did not satisfy all the designers in the business, and even before it reached the zenith of its prosperity alternative layouts were being produced, at first with indifferent success since their steering and comfort were greatly inferior to that of their well-established rivals. However, it was evident that the ordinary was a machine which limited cycling to the young, athletic and expert, and the demand for safer alternatives which required less skill grew steadily.

The 'safety' bicycle may be defined as one with comparatively small wheels, about equal-sized, and a chain and pedal drive to the rear wheel, and such designs, apparently neither patented nor built, can be traced as far back as 1869.

However, H. J. Lawson, in a spirit of experimentation, had actually built one in 1874, and was supposed to have used it a good deal on the roads in the vicinity of Brighton. His researches continued and eventually became productive, but before they did so, Thomas Shergold, a very practical shoemaker of Gloucester, produced a rear-driven machine with the wheels of approximately equal size, chain drive and oil retaining hubs (plate 7). It was much in advance of anything made at that date (1876) and the inventor rode it as far as Birmingham. He offered the design to Starley Brothers in 1880 but it was refused and he advertised it for sale or hire in the local press. Lacking finance or a backer he was unable to develop his ideas and by 1903 he died a disappointed man. His machine is now in the Science Museum. Lawson carried on his experiments with great energy, and after getting on the wrong track for a while with a rather useless lever-driven machine mounting a miniature front wheel, he produced in 1879 a much improved concept which he dubbed the Bicyclette (plate 12), a name immediately adopted in France as referring to bicycles of all kinds.

This design showed distinctly its penny-farthing ancestry with a front wheel much larger than the rear and a single curved backbone from the sloping steering head to the rear forks. The chainwheel was carried in a subframe below and the saddle on a long spring like that of the old boneshakers. Steering was indirect, by means of a coupling rod from the handlebars, which were mounted a foot behind the steering head; altogether an odd-looking hybrid, it was not popular, only a few being made. Evidently Lawson was before his time because the Rover, a similar layout produced six to seven years later, sold well.

In the meantime 'dwarf ordinaries' continued to command the market and it was not until 1884-5 that ' safeties ' became commercially available; even then they had front wheels either considerably larger (Whippet, Rudge, Rover) or considerably smaller (Humber, BSA, McCammon, Star), than the rear. It was evident that the claims of both layouts were evenly balanced and it was not long before the trade settled for equal-sized wheels in the interests of standardisation. Most of the models mentioned continued to have vertical front forks coupled by rods to handlebars mounted well back, but before the end of 1885 Rover (Starley and Sutton) inclined the forks, put the handlebars at the top of the steering stem and made the saddle adjustable. Something vaguely like the modern bicycle was beginning to emerge, but the first form of diamond frame went to the credit of Humbers while

21

McCammon was the first to fit mudguards. The Whippet (Lindley and Biggs) was a spring-frame design with a coil spring in the front stem, and this was good enough to capture some records before the pneumatic tyre made it unnecessary. Nor was it the only spring-frame machine available, others being introduced in 1887-8 by British Star, BSA, Hall and so on. Nobody seemed to want them as *well* as Dunlops.

In the 'cross-frame' Dan Allbone produced in Biggleswade a strong and practical type of structure in 1886. The principle here was that the main tube joining the steering head to the rear forks should be crossed by another tube connecting pedalling gear with saddle (plate 18). The first of Allbone's 'Ivel' cycles were produced for racing purposes and proved most successful; their inventor was a man of original mind, being probably the first to use ball bearings in penny-farthings, while in 1887, by bending the frame tubes, he was able to produce a practical form of ladies' bicycle. In addition, he played a considerable part in developing the tandem bicycle as we know it, with a double diamond frame.

The diamond frame itself was gaining ground in the late eighties, and its advantages in strength and lightness over the cross-frame layouts began to be realised after the appearance of Humber's design, a very primitive-looking form, in 1884. By 1890 this model had been perfected and its layout was almost exactly that which later became universal for over half a century. The first of these machines to come from the factory undertook a journey of fifteen thousand miles which took three years and crossed three continents; the machine concerned is now in the Science Museum.

It was not until about this time that designers turned their attention to the possibility of improving the steering. Inclined steering heads with handlebars mounted on top of the stem had been known since the days of the Cripper, but were far from universal. Many machines were still steered by cumbersome and heavy 'indirect' methods involving levers and rods connecting handlebars to steering stem, and the cross-frame Rudge of 1887 actually had curved front forks, but mounted them pointing rearwards to provide both a castor action and a selling point. By 1890, however, it became generally realised that, for accurate steering, the line of the steering head needs to be aligned with the point of contact of the tyre with the road, and to obtain this the front forks must be curved forwards.

All machines were now fitted with ball bearings but the pneumatic tyre was not yet available. The price of a good bicycle was in the region of £25, or £30 for a racer.

8. PNEUMATIC TYRES: THE TURN OF THE CENTURY

At the Stanley Show, the great annual event of the cycling world, in 1889, an analysis of the exhibits showed 12 per cent to be ordinaries, 54 per cent rear-driven safeties and 27 per cent tricycles. By 1893 the ordinary had vanished, safeties stood at 85 per cent and tricycles had dropped to 6 per cent. For practical purposes all the safeties had diamond frames, chain drive to the rear wheel and equal-sized wheels, nearly all of them with some form of pneumatic tyre.

It is a commonplace that pneumatic tyres provided a foundation for design on which the whole future of motoring was built. Motoring as we know it would be impossible without them. Perhaps this is hardly true to the same extent with the cycle, since thoroughly practical machines were made which did have solid tyres, but the effect of the new invention was fundamental nevertheless; comfort was greatly improved and owing to the lessening of friction, speed was increased. It was found that no solid-tyred racing machine could be pitted against a similar but pneumatic-tyred adversary with any chance of success.

The air-filled tyre had been patented by R. W. Thomson as long ago as 1845, and he had advocated its use not only for carriages but for railways, bathchairs and even rocking-chairs. He conducted tests which indicated a reduction in friction of from 60 per cent upwards but his ideas were never adopted commercially; difficulties of production and a necessarily expensive product killed the idea.

The name always connected with the invention of the pneumatic tyre is of course that of John Boyd Dunlop, a Belfast veterinary surgeon, who took out his first patent in 1888, marketed his tyre soon afterwards, and saw it cause a revolution within two or three years. The invention was made specifically for cycling, the inventor never having been interested in the much larger and more expensive carriage wheels.

The earliest of Dunlop's production tyres were fitted with an inner tube containing the air and an outer cover attached to the rim by cementing and binding. This state of things cannot have lasted long and it was probably the first puncture that directed Dunlop's attention to the need for tyres to be quickly detachable. Within a year several widely divergent types were on the market; the best of them proceeded to win

23

all the races and became universally adopted. The Stanley Show figures indicate the speed at which it happened—percentages were as follows:

	1890	1891	1892	1893
Solid rubber	98	29	4	2
Hollow rubber	1	54	15	15
Pneumatic	1	17	81	83

The tyre secured each side with an endless wire was invented by C. K. Welch and adopted by the Dunlop company; in the first arrangement the sides of the tyre were provided with swellings which were pressed downwards into channels in the sides of the rim, and the wires were secured above them to keep them in place. W. E. Bartlett's design provided thickened edges to the tyre which could be pressed into inward-facing rim grooves, undercut to grip the edges. These two main principles of design later became known as the 'wired on' and the 'beaded edge' respectively, but in the meantime many other types appeared, for example the Preston-Davis wherein the rim bore a number of staples which retained wires in the edges of the outer cover, pulled tight to hook over them on inflation. The Leyland Pneumatic provided the outer cover with studs which fitted into holes in the rim; the Clincher was modelled with a deep well-base having a recess each side for a triangular bead so that half the tyre was buried in the rim; and the Hook tyre, made in Hammersmith, had hooks along the sides of the cover which clipped over the spokes. Other ingenious ideas included the Swindley-Manhole in which the tyre was cemented on and the rim was fitted with a door plate through which the butt-ended inner tube could be withdrawn for repair, and the Boothroyd having outer and inner tyres fabricated as a single unit, canvas enclosed both sides with rubber and repaired by injecting solution into the hole or applying a patch on the outside. Smith's lace-on tyre could be fixed to any rim so that solid-tyred machines could be modernised; Wright's Protector attached small metal scales between tube and cover and claimed to be puncture proof. The Lundgren and the Fleuss employed soft rubber as a sealing for the beads—the original tubeless tyres. The list of ingenious ideas produced in the early nineties seems almost endless but few of them lasted very long and by about 1898 tyre design had become

1. *Hobby-horse or 'Draisienne' of about 1818. Note the adjustable axles: later models had adjustable saddles instead.*

2. *Kirkpatrick Macmillan's design of 1839, the first step forward from the hobby-horse. The original is lost—this is a copy probably made about 1860. It weighs 57lb.*

3. *A rarity: a treadle driven boneshaker probably made about
1865-1868; it seems to have been a painstaking attempt to
apply Macmillan's principles to the Michaux design.*

4. *Boneshaker tandem tricycle. An ingenious design by J. Child of Barnet; the rear rider turns the rear axle by hand, the front brake is applied by a cam turned by the handle-bar.*

5. *The Reynolds and Mays Phantom of 1869, hinged in the middle and the first to have wire spokes in tension. The wooden rims remain.*

6. *The Ariel of 1870, the first attempt to produce a light all-metal bicycle and the first to have spokes tensioned by moving the rim.*

7. *Thomas Shergold produced a rear-driven safety in 1876. The line drawing is by the incomparable Frank Patterson who, starting in 1893, illustrated the world of cycling for nearly sixty years.*

8. *Coventry Tricycle (1878), front steered and with an efficient band brake.*

9. *The Rudge Rotary tricycle with two-wheel steering and chain drive. Made in 1878, the type remained popular for ten years.*

10. *Dan Rudge's quadricycle of 1878, seating two riders side by side. Steering is by both small wheels and there is accommodation for an umbrella.*

11. *The penny-farthing reaches its peak; the magnificent Singer Xtra-ordinary of 1879 with treadle drive and 60-inch wheel. Note the inclined forks.*

12. *The Lawson Safety Bicycle: this was the one called the Bicyclette, Lawson's third and best design. He built it in 1879 but it was not commercially successful.*

13. The rear-steering Cheylesmore tricycle, a popular model made by the Coventry Machinists Co.

14. The remote steering Quadrant tricycle with the front wheel patent mounting from which the firm took its name. The design originated in 1882 but this pneumatic-tyred example looks younger by a decade.

15. J. Boulton demonstrating the 1880 rear-steering Swift tricycle, another popular design.

16. *A dwarf ordinary of Facile type with treadle drive, bought new in 1882 by the father of Miss D. N. Dew, who recently presented it to the Oxfordshire County Museum at Woodstock.*

17. *The Kangaroo of 1884, a dwarf ordinary, driven by a chain and pedal each side of the front wheel.*

18. *An early cross-frame safety of 1885-6 from the remarkable collection of bygones owned by George Swinford of Filkins, Oxfordshire. The machine was bought in Weston-super-Mare and its history is known.*

19. *A Bathchair tandem tricycle by Warwick & Co., Monarch Works, Caversham, Reading, 1890.*

20. *A drawing by Frank Patterson representing an incident in the mid eighties. The para-military suit and pillbox hat were the universal fashion for all riders.*

21. *A rare machine indeed: a pneumatic-tyred ordinary of Geared Facile type with a crypto gear in the front hub. The immediate forerunner of the Bantam, and probably made in 1892-3.*

22. *The Bantam Crypto of 1894, with gearing in the front hub; simple and popular for short journeys.*

23. *A late and improved version of the Crypto-geared Bantam dating from 1896. This was the last of the front wheel drive bicycles.*

24. *The Dursley Pedersen ladies' model of about 1904. Every tube is duplicated and cross braced. Note the hammock seat.*

25. *The Dursley Pedersen de Luxe of about 1904, equipped with hammock seat and Pedersen three-speed hub gear. These machines were usually painted a silver colour.*

26. *A gaslit cycle shop in High Street, Tring, Hertford-shire, probably photographed in the summer of 1904.*

27. *Accommodation for a passenger. An AKD tricycle of 1910 with a basket trailer probably dating from the mid nineties.*

28. *The Sociable tricycle of about 1912-14. A similar design was made in bicycle form!*

standardised, with Dunlop and Michelin as the giants of the industry. The Woods tyre valve, using a tiny piece of rubber tube to trap the air, had been patented in 1891 and was now in universal use. A great deal remained to be done before tyres became really reliable however; rubber mixes were improved and toughened, canvas was laid diagonally and non-skid treads designed. Research on a well-nigh perfect product no doubt continues.

Other refinements

Although as we have seen the bicycle had assumed its familiar shape and proportions by about 1895, this did not mean any slowing down of the flow of new ideas into the industry. Cycling was gaining greatly in popularity every year and the designers realised the imperfections remaining in the products offered to the public. Thought was put into the matter of brake efficiency, change-speed gears and mud-guarding. Roller chains in the form patented by Hans Reynold replaced the old block and double block chains, and it is interesting to see that a shaft-driven bicycle made by Humber and Goddard of Beeston was available as early as 1897, followed by another from Quadrant two years later. Chain-cases had been on the market since the Harrison Carter of 1893, and ladies' machines had dress guards—string networks stretched each side of the rear wheel below the saddle.

A notable happening at this time was the introduction of speed gears, much along the lines which later became so general. Derailleur-type gears, where the driving chain is tensioned by a spring and is caused to jump between rear sprockets of different sizes, were originated by the Protean four-speed gear offered by Lindley and Biggs in 1894, but E. H. Hodgkinson in 1896 produced a simpler design, his three-speed Gradient which developed rapidly into the type we now know. At the same time, hub gear boxes were being patented, the first practical design being the Johnson of 1895, and after this a number of two-speed epicyclic layouts incorporated in the bottom bracket were used until the appearance of the popular Sturmey-Archer hub gear, put into production by the Raleigh company in 1902. It was compact, cheap and light.

Freewheel devices had been available since the eighties and these made essential the fitting of a brake of some kind. Boneshakers, like the wagons of the day, employed a wooden block which pressed on the wheel rim, and when pneumatic tyres came in the idea was resurrected in the form of the 'spoon' brake, whereby clutching the handlebar lever caused a pad to press on the front tyre tread. This was not particularly good for the tyre, but a more serious disadvantage was that any front-tyre puncture rendered the brake useless. For this reason experienced cyclists took care not to have their punctures on steep descents. One attempted improvement used pads bearing on an extra wheel mounted between the pedals next to the chain wheel and dispensed with the free wheel; but although stirrup brakes pulling upwards against the wheel rim itself had been invented for some years they did not become general wear until the turn of the century, after which nearly all the manufacturers fitted them to both wheels.

With the trade set fair for a period of prosperity more factories opened up and the range of machines became considerable, even if their variation in design was much less than it had been. New firms included Elswick, Gale and Son of Reading, and Osmond. The Raleigh concern started when Harold Bowden, riding a cycle for his health, sought out the makers of his machine, Woodhead and Angois, Raleigh Street, Nottingham, became a partner, and soon took over the whole concern, floating the Raleigh Company with a large factory in Russell Street in 1890 and taking on the record-breaking cyclist G. P. Mills as designer and manager. By 1896 the factory had moved to even larger premises in Faraday Road, Lenton, and continued to expand. Dan Rudge's little concern had become the mighty Rudge-Whitworth factory, but his son, who had been employed at Humbers, left to form a partnership with C. Wedge, and manufactured the Rudge-Wedge bicycle in Wolverhampton from 1891; racing models and ladies' machines were included in the catalogue, but for some reason the venture faded out some years later.

Ladies' machines had now become freely available in the early nineties, following Starley's design, and firms specialising in them included Swift, Elswick and Ivel: by the late part of the decade, one machine in three had an open frame. Dan Allbone (Ivel) was also the first to develop and market a double-diamond tandem machine. Raleigh and Humber contended for the tandem market from 1897 onwards, and their layouts provided for ladies, either in front or behind. Freak tandems carrying up to six people were built and even raced in those days; tradesmen's carriers and children's cycles were available from several firms from about 1893 onwards.

9. NECESSITIES AND ACCESSORIES

Until the mid nineties the rider did not really need to purchase anything additional to his machine with the possible exception of a crude oil-lamp, which could be hung on the front spindle of a penny-farthing or mounted above the front wheel of a safety if desired. With the advent of pneumatic tyres however, it was essential to equip oneself with a puncture repair outfit, means of removing the tyre, and a pump. At first this equipment had to be carried on the person and it was not until about 1900 that clips and a leather bag began to be provided on all machines. Tyre pressure gauges could be bought as early as 1893, likewise chain cases—offered mainly with the ladies in mind. The accessory business was getting into its stride. Oil and candle lamps for bicycles had been made since 1880, notably by Joseph Lucas, but the increasing speed and number of bicycles had made a front lamp at least a very desirable fitting for use at night; the law thought so, too. The firm of Lucas reorganised their output accordingly, producing in 1896 an oil-lamp that deserves a paragraph on its own.

It was made to extremely high standards of quality and cost more than most other lamps, but even so it is difficult to understand how it could have been produced profitably at the price. Known as the King of the Road, or in nickel-plated form as the Silver King, it cost 15s 6d. The same article was still listed in the firm's 1940 catalogue at only a shilling more. The lamp was a neat and accurate tinsmith's job requiring a great deal of highly skilled workmanship; the oil reservoir was provided with a filling tube and screwed cap, a glass-covered silver reflector was mounted behind the removable wick holder, the suspension was spring mounted and bore a handwheel to tighten on to the cycle bracket. Coloured faceted lights were provided to port and starboard, the red one opening so that the lamp could be lit in a wind without opening the front. The designer forgot nothing—perfection in front oil lamps had been attained! A mere two years later, in 1898, the company produced what was probably the first available acetylene lamp, made to the same exacting standards; this incorporated the carbide in the base of the light chamber and the water reservoir at the top of the lamp, the whole having a very neat and practical appearance although it was not long before it was radically altered to the later and more familiar form.

Milometers of a kind had been made since the early eighties

but Veeder and other makes were available from 1895 onwards. Coaster hub brakes could be had from about 1900. These were rear hubs incorporating a free wheel and a brake which was applied by pressing backwards on the pedals, thus engaging a small clutch acting on the wheel.

Golden days

The heyday of cycling was undoubtedly between 1895 and about 1902 or 1903. The pastime became a fashionable craze and anyone who desired to keep in the fashion purchased and rode a bicycle. Landed gentry had them brought round to the hall-door as though they were horses; shop girls were proud to do their own polishing and small maintenance jobs. Machines paraded in Hyde Park daily according to the weather, just like the horse addicts on Rotten Row; villages became filled with passing cyclists—the only traffic worth talking about since the growth of the railways emptied the roads fifty years before; the Cyclists Touring Club did great work inspecting and recommending hotels and inns for cyclists' use, advising on routes and repairers, providing maps, road books and periodicals as they had already done for twenty years. Clubs increased in number; as early as 1880 there were seventy-five in London alone.

Few people thought of the bicycle as a means of getting to work—few people indeed in those days lived more than a mile or two from their jobs, and a walk did everybody good. Bicycles were for pleasure, and for those who could afford them. As already said, a large proportion of these were women, and the difficulties resulting from the conventional feminine attire of the day were rapidly overcome in everybody's interest—partly by intelligent design of the bicycle and partly by the appearance of special cycling fashions. Both Gamages and Harrods decided on a whole-hearted support of the movement and both made available not only special clothes for all tastes and weathers, but every conceivable accessory and gadget for the cyclist as well.

Fashion apart, correct clothing for the purpose has always been an important aid to cycling, and this was realised in the early days, even when female ankles were not accustomed to much exposure. A writer of 1893 insists that corsets must be relinquished, and that for underwear there was no substitute for wool. The gown was to be of serge, plain in the skirt so as not to catch in the machinery, with a Norfolk or blouse-cut bodice, Oxford shoes with low heels, suspenders for the stockings ('the pressure of a garter is likely to cause varicose veins'), and a straw sailor hat in summer or small cloth cap in winter. The mentor says nothing about waterproofs, but other experts cunningly suggested sewing loops of elastic on the insides of skirts so that the feet could be passed through them and the skirt kept firmly under control at a low level. All this was a little before the fashion houses caught on to the potential of cycling, and it was not until the last two or three years of the century that Mrs Bloomer's famous nether garment travelled across the Atlantic (not for the first time) to astonish the cyclists of Europe. This consisted of a loose-cut baggy pair of trousers of plus-four type, gathered into thick woollen stockings below the knees, and presumably because they did something to display the previously unseen legs of the female kind, the amount of abuse and invective levelled at the fashion was almost incredible. It was a very practical garment for cycling, especially when worn with leather gaiters, but it never became general wear and had no influence over the fashionable length of the skirt.

Entertainment

Bicycles were now very much a part of ordinary life, and were the subject of many topical allusions. Books were written about them, both fact and fiction; *Three Men on the Bummel* by Jerome K. Jerome is a good example. They figured frequently in circus acts and in the music halls. As early as 1878 the Great Leonati, the 'famous bicycle spiral ascentionist', was amazing the crowds on his boneshaker, pedalling up a rickety-looking helter-skelter arrangement to a vast height; the mid nineties saw the invention of the 'wall of death' on which the original Paoly-Evanos, 'Les Cercles de la Mort', cycled round a vertical circular wall of wooden slats. Trick cyclists (the genuine kind) were to be seen in most of the many circuses.

As an example of what the music halls could do, one may quote from a song of the late nineties:

I've lost my pal, that's why I've got this pal-lor on my
brow,
I used to be a cyc-list, but I'm on the sick-list now.
My Sally rode a Raleigh, and we went out ev'ry day,
But a beast on a Beeston Humber came and stole my love
away.

Chorus

Sally rode a Raleigh, and I journeyed on a Rudge.
I said I'd stick to Sally, and she said she'd never budge.

But Mohawks came and Singers came, and Rovers without
number,
And one fine day, she rode away with a beast on a Beeston
Humber.

. . . Lots of self pity, but no trace of envy. That emotion,
now a mainspring of most international and industrial disputes,
seemed hardly to exist in Victorian days. More cheerful (and
better known) is the contemporary but everlasting 'Daisy,
Daisy . . .'

10. EDWARDIAN TIMES

With the commencement of the new century, an un-
accustomed noise began to be heard on the road—the
irregular stuttering of the horseless carriage and the motor-
assisted bicycle. The latter machines were usually compounded
of an existing bicycle or tricycle on to which a motor had
been clipped by some ingenious enthusiast, and modifications
to the original frame and forks were usually minimal. Motors
waxed rapidly in an atmosphere of hot oil, dust clouds,
barking dogs and general animosity, and became for many
the latest craze which superseded the bicycle. That useful
machine, however, was by now far too well entrenched in
the public affection to suffer any really serious decline, and
people were even beginning to use it for their daily journeys
to work; the fickleness of the fashionable was little loss.

Design had become standardised, even though cycles still
had far to go. They mostly looked like they have looked
ever since; they were fully equipped with diamond frame,
ball bearings throughout, two effective stirrup brakes, good
mudguarding, roller chain drive and, if you wanted it, a
change-speed gear and a chain-case. There did not seem
much left to ask for, and yet it was at this time that one
of the most radically different bicycles ever known was
designed and produced, remaining to win devotees for over
a generation.

This was a design first patented by Mikali Pedersen (who
came from Denmark) in 1893. Manufacture was commenced
at the Beeston works of the Humber Company in 1897 but
by 1902 when this factory closed down a production line was
set up in the Lister Works at Dursley and the machine
became known as the Dursley Pedersen. In place of the
usual lozenge-shaped frame made up out of steel tubing,

46

this design was based on a number of triangles, the triangle being a structure less likely to distort than one with four sides. Each side of the triangles was made up of thin steel rods in pairs, strutted across to provide great lateral rigidity. All structural members were designed to take compressive stresses only and were therefore necessarily without bends or curves. The result was a light and immensely strong arrangement. The saddle was a spring mounted hammock affair, said to be most comfortable, and the whole machine at 26lb weighed a good deal less than most of its contemporaries, besides having a highly distinctive appearance. It was produced in ladies' (plate 24) as well as men's (plate 25) designs, could be fitted with Pedersen's own three-speed gear, and has been called the most scientifically designed bicycle ever to be produced. Output continued until 1914 and a version made by the Stephenson Cantilever Cycle Company was available even after the war.

Other well-known companies continued to produce more orthodox machines, but it was also possible for quite small repair shops to enter the manufacturing business since lugs and fittings of excellent quality could be bought from BSA, Chater Lea, Accles and other firms. Craftsman-made models could thus be had to special order and personal measurement. On the other hand, luxury machines were beginning to make their appearance and the point was made that they could be very good value indeed, since a bicycle was normally destined for many years' use and long-lasting qualities were of great advantage. First the Lea-Francis and later the Sunbeam were manufactured with these principles in mind; they were not light machines but were made extremely smooth running, special attention was paid to the plating and enamel, and they were equipped with every desirable accessory including change-speed gears and chaincases.

The early attempts at motorcycle design and the availability of small 'clip on' engines such as the Minerva, the Clement and the Griffon indirectly did good service to cycle manufacturers, since they showed up design weaknesses in the existing frames, forks, wheels and particularly in the brakes and free-wheel devices which, if they failed on the road as they sometimes did, could have disconcerting effects. Improvements were speedily made although it was not long before motorcycle design went its own way, leaving the bicycle better than before.

Quantity production was receiving serious consideration at that time, and the quality, gauge and composition of steel tubing came in for some research; butt-ended units became available, thickened internally at the ends where the main stresses occur. The Raleigh Company, on their way to becoming the largest bicycle manufacturers in the world, turned over in 1900 to the use of steel stampings for the lugs and brackets in place of the heavy and less reliable malleable iron lugs which had to be cast and machined to size at a cost in time and skill. The new-type lugs were brazed into position by dipping the whole frame in molten brass: strength, reliability and speed of assembly resulted, and the enduring catch-phrase 'the all-steel bicycle' was born. The same firm commenced manufacture of the Sturmey-Archer three-speed hub gear in 1903, in competition with a variety of other designs of two-, three- and four-speed gears already on the market, such as the Eadie and the Villiers.

The shaft drive

A distinctively strange feature of the period was the many efforts to popularise the shaft drive in one form or another. Some quirk of design psychology must have been involved here, since the public had never shown any desire to buy the things except in the smallest numbers, and they could have little or no advantages over guarded chains except that they needed less maintenance (and in any case we know that the majority of cycle chains get no maintenance anyway), and the shaft drive had the serious disadvantages that it was heavy, expensive and involved increased friction, making it invariably harder to pedal. As already stated, shaft drives had been available on several nineteenth-century machines, and among notable firms who attempted to interest the public in them in Edwardian days were Acatène in France, FN in Belgium (several designs at various times), Dürkopp in Germany, Colombia and Pope in America, and in this country Rover and Quadrant. None of them lasted very long in spite of, in some cases, excellent quality.

Several different types of brake were now to be had, and the caliper brake was not long coming out after the invention of Bowden wire. The wheel rims were made with flat sides, and the scissor action of crossed cranks under the pull of the wire closed the brake pads like a pair of jaws. The type is light and powerful and the wheel can be removed without disturbing its adjustment. It is still popular, but never succeeded in supplanting the stirrup brake which is cheaper to produce and needs less maintenance. Coaster hubs with back-pedal brakes continued to be offered, and an expanding-segment brake, incorporated into the hub by a firm called the Chamberlain Patent Brake Syndicate in 1904, paved the way for the internal expanding designs often fitted in later days, and which soon became universal on motor-cars.

The sport was flourishing during this period; Bidlake had organised the first unpaced time trials on public roads, and many specially lightened racing machines were available. It was realised that the most important place for weight saving was in the wheels and this produced a fashion for very small and thin tyres, culminating in the Westwood rim of 1906, designed to take a $1\frac{1}{8}$-inch wired-on tyre. Handlebars were usually of the half dropped type.

1910 saw the Bowden cycle dynamo, driven by a friction wheel pressing against the tyre. This quite supplanted a number of rather clumsy battery sets which had previously been the best electric lighting available. It rapidly became a favourite.

11. RECENT YEARS

When the First World War broke out a number of cyclist battalions were formed, it being the opinion of the strategists at that time that we were in for a war of movement, where mobility would be at a premium. Many of the cycling soldiers were equipped with BSA folding-type machines, very much the same as the ones on which their fathers had trained for the Boer War. They did some good things too, at first, but in the upshot not a great deal of use could be made of them on the Western Front, although in many isolated areas they continued to be very useful for general purposes.

Bicycles were not changed in design as a result of the war, but the rise of new-type cycling clubs wrought a subtle influence, and light sports machines of much more modern aspect came on the market. Look at the Swift ladies' model of 1926 in the Science Museum, with its fully developed caliper brakes, dropout wheels with wingnuts and choice of rear sprockets, its straight tubing and half dropped bars.

It is a truism that what the specialist equips himself with today, the man in the street demands tomorrow, and since cycle racing began to be a sport of considerable importance in the late twenties and much research went into the development of increased efficiency, the results were often incorporated into roadster models a few years later, although in general they were not such as greatly to alter their appearance. However, they did move cycle design out of the stagnation into which to some extent it had fallen during the previous decade. Naturally, many of these new features concerned weight saving, and although some of the materials used for track racing were far too expensive to be commercially acceptable, yet a great deal was done to provide light frames and fittings without loss of strength. The bikes were made altogether more compact, welding and brazing processes were improved so as to require less metal, controls and pedals were made of light alloy, mudguards of aluminium or plastic. New Hudson, in a search for lightness, produced a pressed steel frame in 1936, claimed to have tremendous rigidity; it was assembled by bolting together so that in case of damage, individual members could be very quickly and cheaply replaced —provided of course, that spares were locally available. Meanwhile, racing machines weighed as little as fifteen pounds, employed duralumin extensively in their construction, and had wooden wheel rims with one-inch tyres. They were expensive, but during the early thirties a Hercules roadster or similar could be bought for £3 19s 9d, and an extra 19s 9d would purchase a genuine Raleigh. Better value and greater choice has never been available and accessories in enormous number tempted the cyclist to give his machine an individual appearance with a special pair of mudguards, toe-clips on the pedals to stop the foot from sliding forward, Terry or Lycett saddles with spring or elastic mattress tops, or even clips for a pair of aluminium milk bottles in front of the steering head, just like the road racers.

Tricycles continued to be rare on the roads. They were heavier, more costly and needed a lot of space both in the shed and on the road. Good examples remained available however, for those who wanted them, and this included many active handicapped people who had no choice. There was also a small but enthusiastic band of racing tricyclists, attracted by the completely different handling techniques involved.

British cycles were exported all over the world and were never beaten for quality, even though many other countries produced machines for home sale. An all-bamboo design appeared in the Far East, while France offered the Velocar, on which the rider lay comfortably on his back, thus lessening wind resistance. Tandems were deservedly popular for touring and club riding, and when the team produced their first baby a miniature sidecar was hinge-mounted on the side of the machine, giving complete protection to the captive devotee and not interfering with banking on corners.

The number of the firms in the business had been reducing

steadily over the years, helped of course by the great slump. Manufacture became a highly competitive matter and only the best and cheapest of large-production methods could prevail. The choice of machines available, however, did not suffer, the purchaser still having a great choice of specifications; for instance, three- and four-speed gears could be had with close, medium or wide ratios, and by employing both a derailleur and a hub gear as many as nine speeds could be arranged. This might seem a superfluous luxury for the tourist, but a good selection of close-ratio gears was found essential for time-trials.

The post-Second World War situation produced a rise in prices, petrol rationing, and a flourishing cycle industry concentrated in comparatively few large-scale factories. There was little apparent change in the machines themselves although they were more compact with shorter wheel-base, and increased strength. They had to be strong, for a variety of clip-on motor designs came on the market and any roadster bicycle had to be capable of bearing the strain of a motor producing up to one horsepower, four or five times the strength of the rider, and mounted anywhere on the machine. Bicycles acquitted themselves well and gave very little trouble under the new and exacting conditions preceding the rise of the specially designed 'moped'.

Tandems were mostly of double-diamond frame construction, the 'lady-back' models having been outdated by the willingness of females to use clothing suited to their sport instead of expecting the reverse. Models were not confined to two people, many were made for three or more and (it is hoped, exceptionally) up to a score. A postwar twenty-two seater of 35 feet in length exists in Hampshire for use upon very special occasions, and the *Guinness Book of Records* quotes a thirty-one man 'trigintapede', 50 feet long, in Australia.

12. LATE DEVELOPMENTS

One postwar development remains to be mentioned. The ingenious mind of Sir Alliott Verdon-Roe, the aviation pioneer, considered the possibility of a return to the old cross-frame principle, now that modern metals and techniques were available to make it stronger and lighter than it was in the old days. As was his way, he produced a prototype and gained a good deal of experience; this was in 1946 but no more was heard of the matter, and his work seems to have remained undeveloped until Alex Moulton revived it with new thinking in 1959. His frame was F shaped, with a spine connecting steering head and rear forks, and a seat pillar tube with the pedals at its lower end, and mounted parallel to the steering head. The tubes were flat-sided, oval and tapering. The disadvantages of small wheels for comfort and road-holding were well realised, and, when Moulton decided on their use, his long experience in the rubber industry enabled him to design an efficient rubber suspension system, providing a smooth ride on high-pressure tyres with good steering and less work for the rider. The result was safe and simple: and in addition to that, it looked it. Furthermore, it had an excellent low-level luggage carrying capacity. An effective product of original thinking had arrived, and something of the sort was certainly needed to arrest the decline of the cycle industry, which in 1960 produced only half their 1950 total. Nevertheless, when the invention was first offered to Raleighs, they declined it as commercially worthless and Moulton decided to set up his own production. The machine appeared at the 1962 Earls Court show and, by way of an introduction, one example proceeded to beat the Cardiff-London record by eighteen minutes. Demand overwhelmed production and in 1963 manufacturing space was found in one of the British Motor Corporation factories, encompassing not only the standard type but also a folding model, the 'Stowaway', capable of being dissembled and packed into the boot of a small car in under one minute. Raleighs relented when they bought up the Moulton patents in 1967.

The continuing rise of the motor car and the consequent fear of getting wet except in pursuit of a pastime, has meant a decline in the use of the bicycle for some essential purposes and an increase in the popularity of cycle sports of all kinds. The modern road racing machine weighs under 24lb equipped with a ten-speed gear and a compressed air bottle for tyre inflation. Track machines weigh much less. On the whole it may be said that the sport has developed and improved machines for normal use as well as enabling records to be broken repeatedly; the world speed record for instance, for a car-paced cycle, stands since 1941 at nearly 109 m.p.h.

Road racing or 'time trials' in this country have for many years taken on a peculiarly British aspect, and it is not likely that anything similar to the traditional Tour de France would be successfully organised here. Perhaps this is as well, since the Tour seems often to produce a good deal of hysteria while British racers get on unobtrusively with their early morning work, interfering with nobody. Cycle racing is, of course, dignified these days by inclusion in the Olympic Games, and another aspect of the sport has gained much recent popularity; known as cyclo-cross, it has been organised on the Continent since 1924 but in England only since the Second World War. It consists of riding a given number of circuits over an extremely rough course requiring the competitor to carry his machine as much as to ride it—a spectator sport in amateur and professional classes, and, like most such, more spectacular than useful, but yet one more indication of the continuing popularity of the bicycle itself.

It is likely that cycles are in for a further increase. New roads are bringing more congestion on *all* roads, the traffic problem intensifies, restrictions on the use of cars may be invoked in desperation; anything of the sort would of course be to the advantage of the two-wheeler. Indeed, in some cities in the flatter parts of Europe, the amount of cycle traffic is so great that both cars and pedestrians are sometimes severely held up, but this seems the lesser of two evils, since it allows the movement of more people more quickly before crisis point is reached. There are by-products in health, the saving of resources and the absence of pollution. Cities with a cycle problem are to be envied, and it may be that the time will come when a bicycle is your only possible form of personal transport!

13. INFORMATION

If you are resolved to collect old cycles or to restore one to good condition and running order, you should not normally encounter many snags apart from finding what you want . . . There is little in a bicycle to go wrong which cannot be remedied, and the older machines were in essence either a wheelwright's or a blacksmith's product. Some were nickel-plated in the nineties and this plating will certainly have vanished: most were painted black, and as there were no primers before the days of stove enamelling, the original paint usually drops cleanly off to leave a rusty, evenly pitted surface. There is little merit in restoring such a specimen to look as though it had just left a factory when its very shape proclaims it to be a veteran of thousands of miles and up to a century of snow and blow. Such veterans should be scrupulously cleaned and skilfully painted according to the instruction books, bright parts being nickel-plated at the owner's option.

A good cycle repairer should be able to tackle most things which cannot be done by a good handyman, but be certain that the result bears an authentic appearance in accord with the original design. Wheels are likely to be the weakest part of most veterans and should receive careful attention. If the machine is to be ridden, as much shake or wear as possible should be removed from all bearings, especially the steering. Your specimen will be critically examined by other experts, so you must beware of anachronisms. Spare parts are unlikely to give much trouble; many can be made up, exceptions being the primitive forms of chain and the rims of penny-farthings. Some other rims may be unusable with any modern form of tyre and there may be nothing for it but to rebuild with a more orthodox rim.

Museums

A great many museums include one or two old cycles in their collections, and often these look tragically dusty when some of them might be providing more interest to more people if they were occasionally ridden in local events. Of places where a good collection of historic machines may be seen the following is a representative selection:

Belfast: Transport Museum, Witham Street (telephone: Belfast 51519).

Biggleswade: Shuttleworth Collection, Old Warden Aerodrome (telephone: 076-727288).

Birmingham: Museum of Science and Industry, Newhall Street (telephone: 021-236 1022).

Broadway: Snowshill Manor (National Trust) (telephone: Broadway 2410).

Cheddar: Motor and Transport Museum, The Cliffs.

Coventry: Herbert Museum, Jordan Well (many on application).

Edinburgh: Royal Scottish Museum, Chambers Street (telephone: 031-225 7534).

Glasgow: Museum of Transport, 25 Albert Drive (telephone: 041-423 8000).

Horsham: Horsham Museum, Causeway House (telephone: Horsham 4959).

Leicester: Leicestershire Museum of Technology, Corporation Road (telephone: Leicester 539111).

London: Science Museum, Exhibition Road, South Kensington (telephone: 01-589 6371).

Maidstone: Tyrwhitt-Drake Museum of Carriages, Archbishops Stables, Mill Street (telephone: Maidstone 54497).

Newcastle upon Tyne: Science Museum, Exhibition Park, Great North Road (telephone: Newcastle 815129).

Nottingham: Industrial Museum, Wollaton Park (telephone: Nottingham 284602).

Nottingham: The Raleigh Company's Museum, Lenton Boulevard.

Weston-super-Mare: Museum, Burlington Street (telephone: Weston-super-Mare 21028).

Wrexham: Erddig Hall (National Trust).

Clubs

Anyone seriously interested in the subject would be well advised to join a club; there is usually no obligation to own a cycle and membership will bring opportunities of examining and riding other people's treasures once you have proved able to look after them. There are various private collections about, some of them very large, and the owners sometimes wish their machines to be ridden by responsible club members. Clubs to contact are as follows:

Cyclists' Touring Club (69 Meadrow, Godalming, Surrey). A service to all serious cyclists, providing travel facilities, organised tours, club evenings, legal aid, insurance, a magazine and other privileges.

National Association of Veteran Cycle Clubs. President: C. N. Passey, Benson, Oxfordshire. Secretary: Mrs B. Ellis, Cheylesmore, Carnsgate Road, Long Sutton, Lincolnshire.

Further reading

The Bicycle in Life, Love and Literature; Seamus McGonagle; Pelham, 1968.

Bicycles and Tricycles of the Year 1886; H. H. Griffin; Olicana, 1971.

Bicycling 1874; David and Charles reprint, 1970.

Bicycling—a History; Frederick Alderson; David and Charles, 1972.

Cycles: (I) Historical Review, (II) Descriptive Catalogue; C. F. Caunter; Science Museum, 1958.

Early Bicycles; Philip Sumner; Evelyn. 1966.

King of the Road; Andrew Ritchie; Wildwood House, 1975.

The Story of the Bicycle; John Woodforde; Routledge Kegan Paul, 1970.

Story of the Raleigh Cycle; Gregory H. Bowden; W. H. Allen, 1975.

Wheels within Wheels (The Starleys of Coventry); Geoffrey Williamson; Bles, 1966.

Cycling (weekly); IPC Specialist and Professional Press Ltd.

INDEX